AFTER SHAKESPEARE

for Trude and Milena, with love

AFTER SHAKESPEARE

Desmond Graham

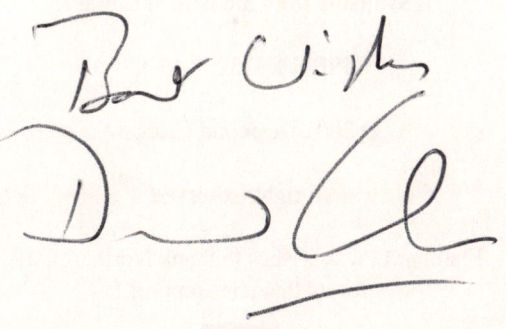

First published in England in 2001 by Flambard Press
Stable Cottage, East Fourstones, Hexham NE47 5DX

Typeset by Harry Novak
Cover photograph by Dominic
Cover design by Gainford Design Associates
Printed in England by Cromwell Press, Trowbridge, Wiltshire

A CIP catalogue record for this book
is available from the British Library.

ISBN 1 873226 45 4

© 2001 Desmond Graham

All rights reserved

Flambard Press wishes to thank Northern Arts
for its financial support.

Website: www.flambardpress.co.uk

Contents

Acknowledgements   7

Prologue: John Gower   9

I
Macbeth   13
Mistress Quickly   14
Prospero   15
Ferdinand   16
Romeo and Juliet   17
Pericles   18
Isabella   19
The Pound of Flesh   20
Perdita   21
Measure for Measure   22

II
Polonius   25
Rosencrantz and Guildenstern   27
Orsino   28
Parolles   29
Sir Toby   30
Beatrice   31
Rosalind   32
Gertrude   33
Portia   34
Bottom   35
Falstaff   36

III
A Wood Near Athens   39
Othello   40
The Mystery of Jack Cade Perhaps   41
Dogberry   42

All's Well That Ends Well	43
Timon	44
Cordelia	45
Mytilene	46
Emilia	47
Barnardine	48

IV

The Doctor	51
Desdemona	53
Apemantus: a Churlish Philosopher	54
Osric	55
Clarence	56
The Duke ('Measure for Measure')	57
Puck	58
Bolingbroke	59
Bardolph and Nym	60
Miranda	61
Kent	62
Imogen	64
Feste	65

V

Ariel	69
Leontes	70
Lear	71
Hamlet	72
Oberon	73
Macbeth II	74
Lady Macbeth	75
Macduff	76
Macduff's Children	77
Lear's Fool	78
Coriolanus	79

Acknowledgements

The first of these Shakespeare poems appeared in my collection *The Lie of Horizons* (Seren, Bridgend 1993): 'Leontes', 'Lear', 'Hamlet', 'Macbeth II' and 'Lady Macbeth'. The idea of a sequence of poems 'From the West End, Newcastle upon Tyne' based on Shakesperean figures came in response to an invitation to contribute 'something on Shakespeare' for a *Festschrift* for Professor Ernst Honigmann. A first group of poems duly appeared in *Shakespearean Continuities* (Macmillan, 1997): 'Prospero', 'Ferdinand', 'Falstaff', 'Lear's Fool' and 'Ariel'. The same year, 'Pericles' was written as a contribution to a Birthday Book for Tony Harrison: *Tony Harrison: Loiner* (Clarendon Press, Oxford 1997). A group of eight poems appeared in my 1999 collection *Not Falling* (Seren, Bridgend): 'Prospero', 'Ferdinand', 'The Pound of Flesh', 'Pericles', 'Measure for Measure', 'Romeo and Juliet', 'Macbeth' and 'Coriolanus'. By now I was working on a book-length collection. I introduced this to the *Shakespeare-Tage* in Bochum in April 2000 and my commentary along with six poems ('Cordelia', 'Timon', 'A Wood Near Athens', 'Orsino', 'Rosalind' and 'Barnardine') was published in the following year's *Shakespeare Jahrbuch* (Munich, 2001). During this time poems had been appearing in magazines: *Antigonish* (Canada), *Ariel* (Canada), *Interpreter's House*, *London Magazine*, *The New Welsh Review*, *North Words*, *Other Poetry*, *Planet*, *The Rialto*, *Southfields*, *Tears in the Fence*, *West Coast* (Glasgow), *Whetstone* (Canada). Poems appeared in differing groupings and with differing titles at different times. I would like to record my thanks to the editors and publishers who first published these poems.

On a personal level I would like to record my gratitude to the late Barry MacSweeney, whose warm encouragement, when I first read the poems locally, greatly helped in the project's completion. I would like to thank Amy Wack of Seren for her continued support, along with Eddy and Isabel Martin, Dr Dieter Wessels, Professor Michael Gassenmeier,

Jack Debney, Michael Rossington and Linda Anderson. To Professor Norbert Platz I owe a special debt for passing the poems to Professor Dieter Mehl, who in turn I must thank for inviting me to read to the Shakespeare Gesellschaft; and to Professor Bob White I owe thanks for years of sharing both Shakespeare and my poems. I would like to thank Margaret and Peter Lewis of Flambard Press for the pleasure of working together again. As with all my writing, the poems owe much to the late Catharine Carver, Gordon and Wilma Meade, and, above all, Trude and Milena, to whom this book is dedicated.

Prologue: John Gower

Where they excavate to show the Roman Wall
and find a prison.

Where the town stopped, gave way to gardens,
five hundred years before.

Where two maids, a cook and butler have been taken over
by ten students, one microwave and a shout from the front door.

Where a Jewish Cemetery has its three graves preserved in a
    Lighting Centre.

Where old terraces which fuelled furnaces of steel for battleships
help the dandelion extend its empire.

Where the Cemetery provides refuge only for the living
and the derelict young.

Where the new Sikh Temple is wired up like a prison,
and the Mosque lets in its light through grids and gratings.

Where Community means the polite young policeman chatting to
the House Agent who later is jailed for fraud.

Where anyone running has stolen something,
anyone sleeping is drunk, anyone standing still
is a visitor, anyone almost undressed
is off for a grand night out.

Where everyone knows having enough money, a bit of time,
a family of sorts, whatever, is everything
and damn nigh impossible, most of all here.

I

Macbeth

He really didn't mean to do it
but now he owns the place,
his shop, called *Hexes*, Gothik
his speciality, anything pierced.
He has four children, all off school;
they practise car theft with Scalextric,
use Nintendo as a system of accounts.
He has a wife or two who sit
in the white Rolls parked against the pavement
and look. Banquo never leaves him;
with a nose and lip ring
he serves the customers and waits.
Sometimes men in plain clothes
climb up the slope, examine merchandise,
declare their love of darkest
porn and videos just to find out.
Macbeth gets on his mobile,
calling up a bunch of lads
dressed up as punters,
black bin liners stuffed
with what they need.
The place is going downhill
since the last shooting,
quick through a pub doorway.
They're running out of pubs
round here to close.

Mistress Quickly

manages *The Waterloo* superbly – she has seen off
with smiles and comfort Hamlet, who would crack
bottles over his head; she has helped poor Cressida
who came in once and stripped off in the corner –
best bra, best knickers – not to be alone;
to her, old Lear, glum and incontinent,
is just an old man needing, sometimes,
to be cleared up. Hotspur has a bar stool
near to the door, in case arguments
flare up. Pistol is her partner. He works
just down the river with the sick and needy.
He listens to their stories, registers their wants.
Just once a week he's here beside her,
with a take-away and a good late film upstairs.

Prospero

He has covered the backs and shoulders
of half the former Gallowgate End
of the *Toon Army* and all the bikers
who sailed with him for the small time,
Prospero – Tattoo Artist;

his designs are legion: dragons wound
round the rib cage, purple tongues of passion
peeping out as snakes between the thighs;
a city side of Calibans he has transformed
with speech in the biceps, pectorals.

On Saturdays in summer you can hear
behind closed curtains sounds of the old days,
Zeppelin, Zappa, a whiff of dope and joss stick
clings to his leathers, a steam of pinks
and purples lights the evening sky.

Miranda long since left him.
Ferdinand wouldn't give a toss
to work for such a wanker.
Gonzalo runs the perfect commonwealth
in the café on the corner.

He has one place left to cover:
the deft left hand he always uses.
The north wind blows a sound
like great waves falling from St James's –
the *Toon Army* is calling for its freedom –

he lifts his implement and we hear buzzing,
the pigeons leave his attic by the broken pane,
right-handed he inscribes a single letter,
'M'.

Ferdinand

Ferdinand paints motor-cycle helmets –
to remind him of his father, at least
that's what Alonso says. In fact
what he saw in the coral – deep sea colour,
movement, nothing in pure light – changed him
forever, and only with an airbrush now
does he care to find his way, drying,
masking, making patterns of the planets,
monsters, spacecraft, Arctic wolf with open jaws.
His gallery is above a bike shop: punters
come daily, haggle about the price.
One day he will set sail with paint,
equipment, and leave this blessed place,
land on an island filled with breadfruit,
pawpaw, avocado, pools of salmon
waiting to be caught, birds sleeping in bushes,
eggs from turkeys boiling in the sun:
and he would spend a lifetime painting it back –
the gold of angelfish, the zebra stripe
of fantail, the lapis lazuli of scales,
the coral shadowed into ruby – all learnt
from Kawasaki, Honda, long days at spraying,
and love of light where you would least expect to find it.

Romeo and Juliet

Romeo still throws sticks
for Buster the pit bull
not worrying that they never reach him;
the broken slide, the seesaw
carpeted with tinfoil, needles;
the swing the Staffordshire tore apart,
its Dunlop Imperial teeth-marked
like its master – Montagues all,
living on handouts, fathers rearing children
like the good Samaritan, mothers
on half time, working nights.

The Capulets live just around the corner.
They have views of hillsides, river:
opening a window brings the whole south in.
They just happen to be there
and with a daughter looking like a picture,
who will land in Cambridge, Oxford,
anywhere, no matter.

He will join his father, brother,
trying to keep that half inch above the water;
and she, one day, in a church vault
will half remember, maybe,
when at four years old, Romeo
told her *I love ye*,
and she understood its truth.

Pericles

He could not stand the land.
There were incidents he talked of
(best forgotten) after the seventh pint
hit him. Something in the chip of light
beyond the north pier looking down
from where Vice Admiral Lord Collingwood
surveyed the river, brought back what?
A rioting of islands? A visit to a king?
His daughter lost to London, found,
and lost again? Or someone he tipped over –
it was rough enough for silence in the human world,
no human voice could break that roaring,
and the one he held and let slip gently
or maybe gave a push to – he will tell it over…
The pavement turns its sickly patterns,
semis passing him in darkness, starboard/
port, starboard/port, starboard/port;
the woman with his fortune in the backroom
off Front Street, spelling the cards; the man
who offered him, unbuttoning her cardigan
across the vinyl, his own wife; and the lunchtimes
drinking where the bars filled up like cabins
and the rats got out long before they sank in silence
through to dreary night: he wanders on,
with seaman's tales of cargoes, landings,
wives in every port and all that stuff,
and then the judder in his talk as if a wave
as high as Collingwood had hit him.
He drifts home staring at the dome of Spanish City,
slipping between the ice-cream stalls to the long tide
still trailing in and waits till its black
has landed – he who sized up Neptune
from the near side, landlocked, longing
for rough weather when you could not think.

Isabella

Sister Mary Bernadetta Isabella
watches the convent garden turn to car park,
stressed steel, double glazing and gazebo
for the *Comfort Homes* for the gently aged,
gazing on pollarded elm and poplar
where the cedars once skimmed off
into infinity beyond the Tyne,
where the slow slope towards the fast outreaches
of the nation's wealth begins its slide.

Sister Mary Bernadetta Isabella hushes
her border collie to the great doors
beaten on by thief and gambler
where today Cyrenians on Sundays
hold their car-boot sale of coffee,
soup and sandwiches, for free,
for a growing cast of thousands.

The Pound of Flesh

The old synagogue turned to photographic
studio, neat vans with logo *Antonio's*
zipping off to all parts piled high with mags;
Salvation Army, closed to visitors except
on Sundays when the silver instruments parade
downhill their tinsel and the abstemious
double-lock large cars; St Paul's,
the school and church set out with razor wire
and double fencing like a prison, the great bells
clockwork; the City Mission, where still the cheapest
cup of tea for miles is drunk by locals
out for the free heating; and that woman,
orange knitted hat pulled tight, check skirt
a sort of marmalade below what once
was herringbone, the thinnest sort of tweed,
a finger on the doorbell, no light upstairs,
but she still looking, waiting for the footfall
and the heavy route to where the signs declare
in front of faded curtains: Spiritualist Church;
and opposite, the Post Office where she queues
each Monday for her pound of flesh.

Perdita

the lost child
lives near here,
platform soles,
PVC trousers,
trying to survive.
No one came to save her
from her island,
her weekly tryst
with the Giro,
looking down to the floral
counterpane crumpled
across the pushchair:
things go on.

Measure for Measure

The police play bowls all summer.
You can hear their shouts *Good wood!*
Good wood! through open windows.
They have blazers blazoned with griffins,
mastodons and auks and look a little lost.
They park their Nissan Stanzas
down by the Deaf Club and check
their locks at intervals and feel
the paint. They go in pairs at least
for it is dangerous in daylight,
and this is not their beat. These
are retired Commissioners, Constables
of Counties, highest Chiefs. Each year
in mufti they see out the long days,
sounds of them clapping after silence
go on through the night.

II

Polonius

was always up
with the latest news;
his counter strewn
with girlie mags and comics,
each day he learnt
The Daily Telegraph
by heart –
he was a touch of class
above us:
the yellowed quiff
and pale beige sideburns
of a cultivated smoker;
the blotched hands
from years of service
in the sun:
he had passed round
Craven A
with kings and consorts;
a slight stoop
pivoted his features,
so his look
was up or down
but never level:
he could tell you
all about Rhodesia
and Enoch Powell
and what was wrong
with Germans.
He disappeared
when everything was over
in the Falklands.
Now Horatio has the shop,
driving in daily
from the country:

you can catch him
sometimes,
just before he puts
the phone down,
chatting surreptitiously
to his wife.

Rosencrantz and Guildenstern

Rosencrantz and Guildenstern: Haberdashery
moved from the main street – a tape
around the shoulders like a priest,
five fingers drumming slowly up and down
the counter's stained brass yard,
they knew the perfect cut.
They could fit you out for funerals
or that extra special day.

Their tweeds and worsteds, double twill
and linen laid out in swathes
or caught in samples, their tower blocks
of buttons once spilling out their contents
like Pandora's other box,
their ready-mades and trial pieces,
hooks and eyes and pins and needles
still wait somewhere for that rainy day.

Now trade has left them. In summer
Rosencrantz stands on the front step,
silent as a shadow, Guildenstern
gazes out the window into empty space.
Their manikins are ageing.
Their hats for every type of weather
pile high like fairground coconuts
in the shadows at the back.

Where once the pins were tight
between their teeth, a soundless
whistle breathes out tunes
no longer heard today.
They could take your measure instantly,
tell size and style and taste, now,
expert in body weight as undertakers,
they can only weigh you up.

Orsino

runs the Post Office
and he'd die for trains –
steam ones, old left-overs
done up in Service Green.
He loves the hiss of steam
on piston, the shrill whistle,
grimy overalls and soot.
You wouldn't know it
as he nods a greeting,
hands across the weekly pittance,
stamps pension books,
collects for light and gas,
but he is far away,
laid back beside his fireman
on the Canadian Pacific,
going up a gradient, one in six.
He is in love
with being on his own
in motion,
surrounded
by the beat and racket
of his engine,
like a conductor
with an orchestra so loud
he is unable to hear,
travelling,
even at a standstill,
anywhere but here.

Parolles

'Pronounce: *Oedipus... Eurydice... Terpsichore...*' –
he would have failed the test to prove he was not spying.
Yet he believes long words, long sentences pay overdrafts.
He believes a wad of papers, details, sums he can't work out
all prove it, the marriage of true minds, his and his customer's –
'Just think of what could happen to your lady wife!'
and he goes over school fees, mortgage, all your father
never thought about, interest, payments, duties,
in a nutshell and he glances past your window
at his Vauxhall Cavalier. He abandoned *The Prudential*
– never really him – the *CGU* when taken over left him on the side.
Now following that widow in the black cape, full-mouthed smile
and everything held in – she must be Helena left millionaire
by Bertram – he is settled. He presses flesh and urges.
'Goodbye my friend, just think about your lady wife'
and he's away to a tableful of paperwork each evening,
spin-dry of customers and microwaves of thought,
lost in his lack of language, his words thrown up like papers
in a twister – the ones his bosses give him show him the way.

Sir Toby

keeps the toy shop. He had been a pilot
with B.O.A.C., still has silvered hair
and skin so smoothed by shaving
he could announce a little turbulence
anywhere. But now he shows his customers
the sign to 'Model Trains' – miles
of Hornby Dublo travelling nowhere upstairs –
there you could buy a sweet shop
for the village by the station
closed down, somewhere in the Dales;
could stock the shop with barley sugar
twists, licorice shoe laces
and sherbert dips; then come downstairs
to all the Airfix kits which won
the Second World War.
He is on board here.
At home he is off the rails.
Sometimes you see Olivia,
rising early in the morning,
pick him up gently from the front step.

Beatrice

lived here once.
She had the repartee to wipe
the shine off toffee, late night
talk to make you wish you never
went to bed. She could take up
a subject, pass it round the table
as if any minute to explode.

Benedick was useless
and she knew, fought him
like a father, with his house
of cards of words, each one
an archway he could blow through
and a single nudge from her
would tumble down.

They were good sports, really –
spent all Christmas sparring
after the first hilarious lock-in.
Beatrice could clean saucepans
with a come-back, flush down
faintest hopes, her shafts of daylight
could plunge through woods
too thick to let another through.

You heard the tinkling of the waves
against her boat side, the rattle
of its stressed steel mast and rigging,
saw the sunshine dazzle of its paint,
not knowing how she dashed
below to check each leaky rivet,
tie tighter everything which rolled,
lash up the wheel which spun
like a propellor where she stood
ankle deep in rising water.

Rosalind

has legs long enough to make it
up the hill before anyone can tell
whether she is man or woman.

Rosalind ties up her hair and back,
puts on a beret, dun coat and ancient
trainers so no one knows her sex.

When Rosalind's at home, alone,
high above street lamps, higher than pigeons
camped in the treetop below,

she lets her hair down like Rapunzel,
all the way, then handful over heavy handful,
climbs back up to reach herself.

Rosalind is a translator, translates
from silence into thought; translates
back all the gabbled chatter

which surrounds her in the daytime
into what it really means: she is mistress
of all languages extending beyond talk.

Then, in the morning, she will lace
her big brown boots, pin up her hair,
and take her whole self with her everywhere.

Gertrude

I suppose she might be Gertrude,
it is hard to tell; bloated face and blousy,
mobile breasts you could have seen tremble
behind organza between the wars.

Actually she looks poorly,
stumbling over every step
as if her heels had listed,
one to starboard, one to port.

Without those eyes which flash
some meaning, she would have looked
at home behind a Gin-and-It
wrapped in fingernails on fire.

She has a silence which she bustles
down the street with, small and close
inside her, but it's her own
and no one can come in;

she takes it to the station,
takes it on and out to sea,
or sits alone with it each evening
catching the faces she can recognise on TV.

Portia

has a pilot's licence,
has a private plane;
turns old hovels
into model buildings
charges a fair rent;
her tenants for the most part
play the cello, paint self-portraits,
translate Rilke from the French;
her partner is a pacifist
who just missed prison
by living in a cave;
she sorts out parking feuds
of neighbours,
dreams of Belmont
where their yacht is moored:
they have no time to get there –
he must practise every day,
he is champion of accordion
since 1954.

Bottom

Bottom writes poetry, he likes it epic best.
He doesn't live here, has a string of garages
down by the Tyne, but they're just on the side.
He has a place in Corfu. Two weeks at every Christmas
he goes scuba diving off St Kitts but it's his poetry
sustains him. To see him shark-suited,
selling a Volvo, popping on the train,
First Class, you would not know
that sonnets are his playthings, elegies
the kind of thing he'd like to read
in bed. Shakespeare is his favourite,
Brooke and Masefield, seekers after beauty
like himself. It's just illusion if you see him
of a Friday, BMW parked outside *Godfather's*,
bouncers giving it a glare: what he would choose
would be to lift his Parker, shake his cuff-links,
scribble on all night. Ever let him know you do a bit yourself
sometimes and he will trap you in a corner, read and read
and read his silvered verses, ask you how to find
a publisher, not even think to buy a pint.

Falstaff

Falstaff knows what honour is
he works at a University.
His special interest is poetry
against war. He lives high
above the city where once
he memorised the name
of every pub by heart.
He is growing older.
The Haymarket has been made
a car park, *The Bay Horse*
struck down by a single
shot. *The Farmers Rest*
was broken to make way
for Marks and Spencer,
only *The Hotspur* carries on
all huff and puff in yellow chalk
on blackboards and at such a price.
He is mindful of the ending
written for him by his master,
keeps away from placemen,
anyone who believes in rising
other than in bed or,
just possibly, from dead.

III

III

A Wood Near Athens
(A Midsummer Night's Dream)

That patch of grass between the houses,
'square' they call it, is a wood near Athens:
here nightly youngsters change to beasts,
bellow into darkness, roar. It has visitors all summer
down from Scotland on an ancient route,
clutching their white cider, all they have and hold.
You can watch them as they pass the bottle,
tottering and making gestures broad enough
to be a shadow play: there's Pyramus,
naked to the waist, his fly gaped open;
there's Thisbe, with skirts enough
to hide the lot of them from rain;
there's Wall, poleaxed beside the bench
they used to make that fire. A little later
local sprites and fairies come and crouch
over flames and foil, inhaling magic:
midsummer night and it's light enough
to watch them right through to morning,
see how they fall asleep and dream.

Othello

flicks his left leg forwards as he walks:
he looks like James Mason after the fire
caught Rochester, not really black;
but he's no actor, merely noble,
with a lined face from lack of sleep
and far too many tranquillizers
they thought would help.

He greets you like a monarch
as he leans against a shop front,
gathering his breath.
He is always in his best, trim
and courtly, gracious as he nods
a greeting, stumps on past.

He keeps no company,
finds no need to talk of anything
beyond the brightness or the greyness
of the day, a Duke of York
who marches up the hill
and down again each day.

The Mystery of Jack Cade Perhaps

Was it Jack Cade's confrères?
She with the circular-saw voice,
armband, spangles falling onto her chest;
he with red eagle on one bicep, lightning
on the other; or he with lifetime's
stubble gracing grey cheeks;
or that natty one, Jack, naturally,
neat faced and smoking a roll-up made
to measure, bright as a roman candle.

They talk with riotous abandon.
'I'll train to be Probation Officer.'
'You see!' he tore the top off the beer mat,
writing it down. 'Do you know this?'
to silence – the beer mat slipped in
the back pocket of his jeans. And she,
strident as Trident cut in half at Rosyth,
'Don't talk about my body' –

it was all over the place, the wall, table
and, soon to be, the floor; and from the stubble:
'You see this film,' drowned with bar noise,
some juke box, laughter, shouting for a pint;
and some time later, he, after, 'We drank
Curaçao and Martinis,' the stubbled one,
Jack Cade no doubt, stirring it up:
'You see when a book ends, it mustn't say,
you mustn't know, a mystery'; and it was.

Dogberry

is very tall, not old at all –
his words may be that bit
caught in the mixer,

his steps, even –
he trips a little
as if made for flatter land.

He knows what happens.
He sees what comes and goes.
He helps small children

shuffling at the lights:
but his words,
after that greeting, *Hi'Ye*,

often falter – you ask him
how was his one day off this summer
and three buses will have taken up

and left again before his start.
From the far side
his right hand raised

is more than blessing,
greeting far deeper
than the tricks of speech,

deeper than the problems
of getting through a sentence
intact. He is bigger

than a giant and gentler
than bread-and-butter pudding
waiting on a plate.

All's Well That Ends Well

Helena, in a baseball cap reversed,
goes uphill along the pavement,
belted coat and battered trainers,
stares ahead with purpose;

Bertram, behind a pram piled high
and overboard with full bin liners,
steps uphill ahead of traffic,
brisk and hardly bending:

they move like man and dog who know
so well you can't tell which would need
the lead if lead were needed:
she could be dental nurse

to his brusque surgeon, he could be
trolley-man to her consultant;
five yards apart, they hold each other up
as if an iron bar between them.

They spend each day before the rush
of people, after everything has quieted
to a cold November, deft as someone clearing
after children, picking through the bins,

early birds of the half dusk,
keeping up appearances, hoping
if they move on fast enough
nobody will see them.

Timon

He keeps undressing – no one quite knows why.
He starts with jackets, two of them, for he has both
an old tweed from a teacher and a lumberjack affair
now turned a plaid of holes. You think he's seeking
something, fingering the pockets, sleeves
and corners, opening the front, and then the next one.

It's like an old man dressing slowly, played backwards:
jackets off, now shirt, now vest and it is easy –
he is gently pulling at his belt, the jeans
fall simply, nestle above scored boots.

There's nothing vulgar, dirty, just an old man
in the buff. The boots come off, no socks,
and then he drags each trouser leg, a chrysalis
case, to show the cabbage white of legs.

He would peel off his skin if she would let him,
holding his clothes like a trainer by a track
or his own mother when she bathed him
and he was ankle deep in steaming water.

He has nothing more to lose and nowhere else
to look. He takes his clothes and holds them
like a patient finished with the doctor,
tactfully, in the right place. She helps him put them on.

Cordelia

has grown fat.
She has a little troop of followers
she picks up where they lie,
she is barrel-strong on the pavement,
loud as sirens on a Sunday,
bellows at the slightest threat,
she will defend them
from the small boys who spit
into their bottles, the men
who make them leap
out of their skins, and anyone
who looks with curiosity
on their pantomime of standing up:
one glance from years in the wilderness
withers you up; and then, again, she's mother,
husband, father, to her silent crew –
except for one of them, the gangling
loner who occasionally tagged on,
went where she would never venture,
was murdered in the street.

Mytilene
(Pericles)

The back lane is lined
with black bin liners
torn apart by tramps –
tea bags, beer cans, chicken bones,
pasta pigeons brought to light –
but this is full of phials
and needles, cartons, packets
of their trade. They peer
all day behind the curtains,
barely turn as Busies
climb their steps and knock:
they have their friends
and know their faces;
young girls off school
pop in and stay a while,
men with ink tattoos
give each one a mouthful
as they leave the steps.
They speak to no one
yet their house is full.
This is where Marina
must have landed
years back and never left.

Emilia

writes behind a doorslam,
her notation is in decibels of scream,
how hard the walls are beaten by what fists.

Sometimes she looks down at the map of troubles
on her skin: most times she is silent,
just a quick-fire word when asked.

She has been blamed for hearing keyholes
open, cursed for knowing just the time
the walls caved in. She specialises in silence,

silence broken, silence prolonged
long past the time it should have been,
silence between lips trembling,

silence as she turns the other way.
One night she jumped up, shouted,
opened up and called to know

what happened – she had her say,
left it perched above the silence
like a pigeon on a building just falling in.

Barnardine

keeps slipping out each time
I take my pen up.
He hears computers
long before they're on.

He shuffles up blank pages,
makes sure you find him
when you're out of ink.

I tried to write him
but he lay there
burped and farted,
turned over for another drink.

Three times, like Peter,
he was summoned
and without a cock to crow
or even sirens
he sloped off without a word.

I can see him now, flat out
between the roadworks,
paramedics bent
like supplicants to Christ

and that pale look
you see in Resurrections
stained right across his face:

He phoned the Fire Brigade
three times then lit the fire
to call them. This time
he breathed in too much smoke.

IV

The Doctor

who saved Lear
with a potion,
sent him to sleep,
unwittingly saving him
for so much worse,
is really an optician.

He has a shop behind closed
doors and windows,
without a nameplate, buzzer,
yet he's always open:
all you have to do
is walk right in.

He works upstairs,
behind five flights
of boxes, bundles,
treasure chests
of measurements
for everybody's need.

He has an old chair
like a dentist's,
with the leathered
wood arms
of a veteran,
holding you up.

He has a board
with letters so big,
you know you will be well.
Downstairs his young assistant
whistles quietly,
leaving you alone

and like bare woodland
transformed into a place
for feasting, sparse cabinets
unfold their sides,
table tops turn over
onto a paradise of frames.

His customers are rarely
under eighty.
He helps them read
the small print, see through
the magic eye
in the door frame

who has called.
And when he finds your lenses,
slots them in,
you understand
how people felt
whom Jesus cured.

Desdemona

Behind the rows of Prince Albert
flat-backed Victorian stoneware,
the ashtrays with Union flag, 1901,
jade brooches spelling *Beulah*,
jade buckles, bugles, the fish-green
saucer with what looks like toe-prints
(Maling) and a pink fruit bowl
it would be criminal to cover,
an empty glove of amber, spode,

she sits behind this daily,
opening to morning
beside the saw repairers
and the dealer in safes,
her yorkie settling at the far end
on the prie-dieu with picked out
Flanders lace; she chainsmokes,
rising only to replace the ashtray,
never reads:

        at evening Emilia
calls her, steps outside and waits:
she draws out the iron bars
taller than herself and slots them in
at corners, heaves up a cross piece,
padlocks, bolts and levers,
turns the whole place back into a prison
which she leaves until next day.

Apemantus: a Churlish Philosopher

Chin up, throat out, eyes fixed on something
twenty yards ahead, he sidles up the hill
at speed, nose just above the water like a snake.

He will snarl with a flare of nostrils
like a charger out of Delacroix; curse
with the slow lowering of his pint.

He will burst back through the toilet doors
as if entering a Western, bar-tender
canoning him a drink. His greeting is a silent

splutter. His farewell a Prussian Major
Domo's click of the cheek bones, slope
arms of the jawline, about turn, and off.

Osric

guards the stage door.
He can change sex in mid-
sentence, use a lisp as if
he planed down words
to fit a glove compartment,
glance aggression
as a game of hide and seek.

He greets you frankly,
adds a joke that festers
as it falls without a laugh,
picks up silence like lights
around a stripper,
plunges you in darkness
with his every witty word.

Teenies who come for dancing
show him steps they're shy about
with mother. Aspiring Groups
swop stories of their triumphs
getting laid. Big names he drops
with condescension. Every time
you leave, he looks dismayed.

Clarence

runs *The Diving Centre*.
He had this dream. Now he fills his windows
with models in rubber suits and flippers,
masked so you cannot see the face;
there is a black boat, twin-engined,
marked with transfers like a bomber –
'Blonde Bombshell', anchors, how many divers
will go on down. A cardboard cut-out
guards the entrance like a target,
its crooked left elbow points the way
to the new bridge controlled by cameras
looking for the newest breed of youngsters
playing chicken every day. The cellars
are bricked up against flooding. The ground floor
rots below its cladding. The roofs leak tiles
onto the paving. Soon, the south-bound tide
of traffic will wash straight through this doorway.
Clarence mounts his Opel Charger,
adjusts his seaside tie and drives away.

The Duke
(Measure for Measure)

drives a Jaguar
sometimes, sometimes a Porsche.
He has business in Botswana
which takes him, often, away.
He owns the *Golden Lotus
Take-away*, you can hear
his customers, ink tattoos
on their fingers, cigarettes
behind their backs,
comparing jobs and sentences
and crimes of others
far too horrible for them to do.
He has a satellite in the garden
to pick up porn and news,
a girlfriend in the basement,
on the internet all day,
at night, he goes disguised
in darkness – in the morning,
envelopes for Amnesty
International litter our mats.

Puck

would be the devil, really,
he dresses up in red and waves a candle
like a thunderbolt through dark.

He has accomplices on stilts,
grim-faced in masks from science-fiction,
garlanded in gowns and black.

With his wand, whole unicorns
burst into flame, lion heads
shoot fireballs through their sockets.

He is the master of his ceremonies,
each year lights up our dull November
with his carnival of fire.

Spanish Inquisitors would have loved
his pyrotechnics; stage designers
could have learnt a trick or two

but his heraldic beasts and drummers,
his wild companions, flaming wheels
and arches made of fire,

and his own torch which lights up
everything in stages, is all forsaken
magic with no place to go,

picked up and flung about like music
from a great composer born
generations after his time.

Bolingbroke

tried to join the police force
but failed:
never answered questions
unless he knew the truth.

I've seen him lift up by the lapels
a man soliloquising
into an unpaid drink
and throw him out.

His shave, his signet ring,
his little waist,
his lack of sideburns, gleaming
watch strap, hold him up

and two blondes, expert
in drinking slowly, dangling
an ankle under a bar stool,
and synchronised laughter.

Bardolph and Nym

stand half the summer
propping up the doorposts,
naked to the waist,
spend winter deep
in their workshop
breaking bikes.
They live for Fridays
and a night out
by the river,
miniatures of Budweiser
three pounds a shot,
the noise too loud
to shout through,
jam-packed
as in disaster movies
as the ship goes down:
pulling the birds,
they call it,
and they know a bouncer
where they get straight in
for nothing –
never remember
whatever happens next.

Miranda

serves cappuccino
at *The Alchemist*, Pink Lane;
she made it up from London
to where wicker chairs and tables
fill up with traffic from the station,
sprinkles milk with chocolate,
tries to read a message on the top.

Her father trawls the local papers
for her name. She spells the cards
for her decision – Corfu,
Katmandu or Casablanca?

Each night she lifts the sash cord,
leans her top half out as if a mermaid,
listens for the sea – it is only diesels
with night mail heading south.

Kent

(i.m. Big Hec)

has buckets, balanced
like a milkmaid's, filled
with coins – he collects
for children – shakes them
with a thunderclap of resurrection
as he comes in.

The bar staff always know him;
punters pass the time of day –
he tells them: laid low last week
with flat feet, bunions,
his giant heart missing a beat,
his pulse, his kidneys –

and he pulls a face
like a comic jailor
talking of Death Row.
He is always in the papers
and he shows you, clippings
scuffed with handing round.

He stands there sweating like a mountain
with the first hot sun,
in boots from underneath the beanstalk
where he rescued Jack.
He has a smile as big as saucers
and he sinks a pint like sand.

Some said he siphoned off
his takings for a living:
his flat was ransacked
in a hunt for treasure
or simply out of hate
because he really cared.

This year the children
will go without his calling,
his counted pence wrapped up
and turned to shrieks of joy:
last time his place was broken into,
his heart gave way.

Imogen

She landed, perhaps from a moonship,
perhaps from a Tardis, landed
once they dug the road up for the new BT,

no one heard talk of her till she appeared
then, sturdy in rompers and bundled in pampers,
she strode to her mother not saying a word,

just a look up like dead Cleopatra
and the tables were turned: she ran the place
with a rod of flowering currant, a rule of gardenia,

magnolia blossomed in everything she said;
she rode over the sand dunes, the child slopes of ridges,
the lingering waves at the edge of the sea;

a flick of the finger, flash from her lapis blue eyes
and they did it: not battles and things, just clearing up,
getting on with the story, ready
to be in the right place when it ended.

Feste

skis in the Cairngorms and he is seventy or more,
runs a Mini Cooper, pillar box red, GT,
has an attic flat with a backroom stove
with kettle always on, whistling winter away.

His front room is a bar from summer somewhere,
Acapulco on the ashtrays, Taormina on your glass;
sun sets over Hong Kong harbour right across one wall,
flamingos in the Serengeti take off beside your head;

the fireplace overflows with tiny rickshaws, castanets
and dolls in cerise lace. He knows long before your glass
is empty, and can move with such a grace, your whisky
becomes Ginger Rogers to his Fred Astaire.

Here Christmas is in Rio, Boxing Day in Martinique,
and the sharp north wind, the driving rain,
can do their worst outside, all week.

V

Ariel

Ariel is an editor.
He counts the pages
to his great escape.
He has no wish to join
the drunken butler.
Caliban, his colleague,
really drives him mad.
But he is tired.
He wants to work his magic
entirely for himself.
He has stretched a footnote
through three pages,
started up at midnight
to preserve a single letter,
drifted through an evening
over one full stop.
But Prospero is almost done
with books: now Ariel
will lift his pen and write,
of what? How when he swung
his legs between the boughs
of metaphor and fact
Propsero had thought him
trapped? How once, on an island,
ink through bone of feather,
hot lead pressed down,
sleet in casual patterns
on a lighted screen
all made their passing mark?
Ariel yawns, stretches out a foot,
scuffs out the fire
and one by one,
practised as a midwife,
picks out Prospero's
half-burnt books…

Leontes

is pushing a pram up a hill
talking to the cushion
plumped up inside.
He wears a suit too small for him,
frayed at collar and cuffs
and a little greasy.
He is alright, really,
just a bit abstracted.
Sometimes you see him with a woman,
stockings round her ankles,
tottering in heels,
just a thin blouse
though it is winter.
They are walking down the same hill
with the same pram
with the cushion in it,
talking.

Lear

carries everything he owns
about him, a toppling coat-stand,
overcoats humped on his back,
anoraks and jumpers
padding out his front
like a stage fat man.
He has a belt of washing line
hung with bags and bundles;
in each hand holdalls and carriers
weigh him down. He moves like a boulder
in slow motion. No one bothers him,
not even children.
He says nothing.

Hamlet

is tall and thin, with stubble
and those spectacles snapped off
at one side and taped with plaster
over the nosepiece. The first time
I met him he was crying,
told me about his father,
could not be consoled:
to see a grown man in the street
dribbling and crying,
jacket stained with tears –
he lives round here:
I've seen him often since,
begging.

Oberon

Oberon would like to run the show,
his cloak alone would take anyone in,
his merest word would whisk up cloud
and make a thunderstorm to change the lot of them
or strike down wrongdoers in a flash:

he would sit back like Jupiter
in the old stories, flinging his darts,
one arm round Titania, the other with a glass
pink-coloured, bubbling, swallowed
and refilled at once by little toddlers in fur.

But he is fuddled, frowsy, out of luck.
All he does bounces off the bonnets of their
speeding cars, gets flung back by shaven-
headed lapiths or knocked flat. His words
are just sky-writing to their swirling sprays.

He huddles up at evening, looking like a saint
whose prayers have met the stony ground,
the tares and bindweed swallow up his crop:
charming, voluble and free, ready to fly
anywhere, he must start again and see

he's out of work, he'll have to be retrained,
his magic skills transferred to wishing, an ability
to hope, a way of seeing something in nothing,
be just the bloke to keep the bar staff happy,
see clouds with silver linings, the dead always on the up.

Macbeth II

Macbeth shadow boxes through the afternoons
in the covered market; he likes to do it
by the butcher's best: their great carcasses
hung up on gibbets, pigs' heads on a dish:
he'll be there, bobbing and feinting,
dabbing out an elbow, beer can in his fist;
and all the time a kind of talking,
gibberish in grunts and exclamations,
insults, invective, volleys of abuse
and not a word of sense among them:
the butcher boys put down their knives,
lean back and listen as he weaves on past:
another drop of shoulder, left jab, shuffle,
another burst of taunts, commands and threats,
none of it intelligible, nothing.

Lady Macbeth

Unbelievably in a shocking pink
mini, orange hair cropped,
no expense spared,
tiny as a ballerina
and past fifty,
green stilettos,
pale green stockings
and a lemon jacket,
brand new metal suitcase,
bags of make-up,
artificial suntan,
she swings the case
to shoulder height
as anyone draws near,
snarls a threat
and stares right through them,
focussed,
terrifyingly,
on someone else not there.

Macduff

tried to call his wife,
his child, his children,
but the phone was cut;
he was in London,
he called a friend,
a lawyer, someone in the know,
and shouted, but it made no sense:

he travelled back that evening,
last train,
arrived at Central Station
to a life laid waste;

he wrote letters,
talked to Furies,
placed posies of flowers
by every wall;

a little later he was found
by the railway line
near Cramlington,
just bent over
as he almost leapt
or maybe held back
just a little.

Macduff's Children

In a cage made out of one arm from a playpen
wedged between crates and boxes and two walls,
the children, dribbling, eyes aged,
like two dogs who had been terribly brought up,
cannot find a way to play. One stands, leaning
on the rail of the playpen, any minute to be told
to get back down. The other sits as if ambushed
in the corner, waiting to be told to get back up.
A man at the front is perched uncomfortably
on a stool covered in rags. A woman beside him
wonders whoever has wandered in:
they have a few things in the window,
lost or found or come by, nothing worth much.
These are the last poor edges of what lives
when darkness is pulled down
with a mouth and someone's features,
and you cannot see through.

Lear's Fool

took to evenings
by an old piano, singing along,
his black dog beside him:
with morning he was at the convent gates,
a cough outside and the grill
slid back upon his mug of tea.
His black dog never left him:
all summer long they rolled through
the long grass just like children,
and in winter walked a pace
apart without a word or whistle.
The dog, through good food,
slowly thickened; the Fool
stayed thin enough to slip
through railings, brimful
of courtesy and silence.

Coriolanus

Coriolanus never comes:
sometimes you see his handiwork
in *The Chronicle* – someone in hospital,
a corpse; he runs things
his way, has a way with people,
foot soldiers of his mutilate
and kill; he is a man of honour
and decision: his only vice,
as he says, is success.
Meanwhile, whole streets in Elswick
are dedicated to not talking,
not even waiting for the knock,
pensioners who rummage through the dustbins,
children who will never go to school:
that's how things are and he, for one,
just cannot understand the fuss.